KT-563-128

TRY THIS

A fear of water can hold many people back from learning to swim. If you are nervous to get in the pool, don't worry, you're not alone. Plenty of people learn to swim in their teenage or adult years. Start by getting your feet wet and then gradually get deeper into the water. When you can stand in water deep enough to put your head under, try holding your breath under the water and then breathe out by blowing bubbles. Hold the side and practise kicking with your body stretched out. Wearing goggles can help build confidence under water, too.

Many swimmers find they also get other benefits from swimming. They develop life skills such as sportsmanship, time management, self-discipline, goal setting and a greater sense of self-worth.

Entering swimming competitions can be fun and you may even win a trophy! It's interesting to see how fast you are compared to the other swimmers.

SWIMMING WARM-UPS

Before you start your swimming session, you need to know your body is ready for the challenges ahead. Warming up is essential.

As swimming is an all-body workout, try to stretch all of the major muscle groups before you swim. Gently swim for five minutes before doing your stretches so your muscles have had a chance to warm up. Hold each stretch for 10 to 15 seconds, and run through this routine three times. Once you've completed your warm-up, start swimming slowly at first. Don't try a really fast length until you have done several gentle ones.

Leg stretches and shoulder stretches like these help your muscles warm up.

GET ACTIVE!

LIBRARIES NI
WITHDRAWN FROM STOCK

SWIMMING

Alix Wood

WAYLAND
www.waylandbooks.co.uk

All sports can be dangerous. Do not attempt any of the skills in this book without supervision from a trained adult expert.

Wayland
First Published in Great Britain in 2019 by Wayland.

Copyright © Hodder & Stoughton

Published by permission of Gareth Stevens Publishing, New York, NY, USA.

All rights reserved. No part of this publication may be reproduced, stored in a retrieval system, or transmitted in any form or by any means, electronic, mechanical photocopying, sound recording, or otherwise, without the prior written permission of Wayland (a part of Hodder & Stoughton).

Produced for Wayland by Alix Wood
Picture and content research: Kevin Wood
Editor: Eloise Macgregor
Editor for Gareth Stevens: Kerri O'Donnell
Consultants: Denise Ward and Matthew Stacey, Devonport Royal Swimming Association

HB ISBN: 978 1 5263 1172 6
PB ISBN: 978 1 5263 1173 3

Photo credits:
Cover, 1, 3, 4, 5, 6, 7, 8, 9 bottom, 22, 24, 28 © Shutterstock; 29 © Mitch Gunn/Shutterstock; 9 top © Cpl. J. Gage Karwick/defense.mil; all other photos © Greg Dennis.

Acknowledgments
With grateful thanks to swimmers Alex Christie, Georgia McCay, Jamie Bailey, Liam Ward Nathan Gallagher, Rachel Ward and Rhiannon Davies.

Printed in China

Wayland
An imprint of
Hachette Children's Group
Part of Hodder & Stoughton
Carmelite House
50 Victoria Embankment
London EC4Y 0DZ

An Hachette UK Comany
www.hachette.co.uk
www.hachettechildrens.co.uk

CONTENTS

Why Swim? 4

Swimming Warm-ups...................... 6

The Strokes.................................... 8

Starts and Turns........................... 18

Lifesaving 22

Water Polo....................................24

Try Diving.....................................28

Glossary 30

For More Information 31

Index...32

WHY SWIM?

Swimming is good exercise. It works almost all of the muscles in the body. Swimming develops strength, cardiovascular fitness and endurance.

Once you can swim well you can take part in a lot of other activites, too. Surfing, canoeing, waterskiing and windsurfing are all sports you should only really do if you are a confident swimmer. You can swim for fun, to enter competitions and to help you take part in other water sports. Strong swimmers can become lifeguards, too, once they have learnt lifesaving skills.

Swimming is fun, and it could even save your life. It's a great idea to learn to swim well.

TRY THIS

To get your body used to cold water swimming, try taking cold showers or wear light clothing in cooler weather. Gradually you can train your body to get used to the cold.

Water draws heat from our bodies faster than air. This is why a water temperature of around 15.5° C can lead to **hypothermia** while a similar air temperature feels warm. Open water swimming can be especially cold and dangerous. Signs of hypothermia include violent shivering followed by a lack of shivering, slurred speech, numbness and difficulty thinking straight. These are all signs that you should get out and warm up! You should also cool down after a swimming session. This helps clear waste products from the muscles. You can do this in a warm shower, holding each stretch for 30 to 40 seconds.

Stretching, walking or skipping are good ways to cool down. If you just sit down after swimming you will stiffen up.

THE STROKES

There are different swimming strokes, which can be useful for different things. If you want to swim fast, front crawl is best. If you would rather glide silently through the water on a secret mission, sidestroke is the one for you!

The main strokes used in swimming competitions are front crawl, breaststroke, backstroke and butterfly. There are other swimming strokes, too. The trudgen is like front crawl except the legs do a scissor kick. Many people do the doggy paddle when they first start to swim. The doggy paddle uses the hands in a downwards motion, a bit like how the paws of a dog move when it swims.

This young girl is doing a doggy paddle.

Treading water is a swimming technique to keep you above the surface for a long time without using a lot of energy. A survival travel stroke is a slow stroke that can be done for long periods. The person alternates their arm strokes so that one moves them through the water while the other one lifts them up in the water.

TRY THIS

To do sidestroke, lie on your right side in the water. Stretch out your right arm with your hand on its edge so it slices through the water. The left arm lies across the chest. The right leg does most of the kicking. You must kick, sweep the right arm around and then do a small sweep with the left arm. You can change sides when one side gets tired.

Navy SEALs doing lifesaving training using the combat sidestroke

The combat sidestroke uses little energy, so it allows swimmers to swim for a long time. With barely any noise or splash, it also makes the swimmer less visible. This stroke is used by the US Navy SEALs on missions.

In most swimming races, swimmers compete against each other using the same stroke. A **freestyle** swimming competition allows the competitors to chose their stroke. The stroke almost everyone choses is front crawl, as this style is generally the fastest.

Breaststroke

Breaststroke is popular with people who like to swim for fitness. It is the slowest stroke, but it can be swum powerfully and at speed.

When doing breaststroke, keep your body level and your shoulders in line. Your hips need to be flat in the water. Your feet and legs move **symmetrically**.

Stretch your arms out in front of you, just under the surface of the water.

Then press both hands out to just past your shoulders. Bring your arms around to draw a full circle.

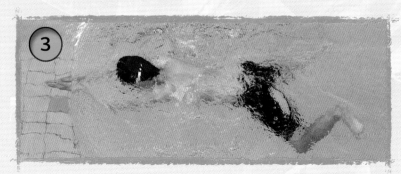

Stretch your hands forwards again. Your arms and legs should stay under the water. Kick with your legs.

Breathe in as you finish the circle, lifting your face out of the water.

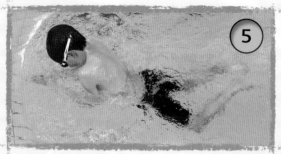

Bring your shoulders out of the water, and then repeat all the steps again.

TRY THIS

Try to practice your leg movements sitting on the side of the pool with your legs dangling in the water.

- bend your knees and bring your feet up
- turn your feet out so that you can push back with the bottom of your foot
- move your feet out and in again to meet each other
- straighten your legs with your knees touching
- try to practise this in the water, too. Hold on to the side with your legs stretched out behind you and try the movements

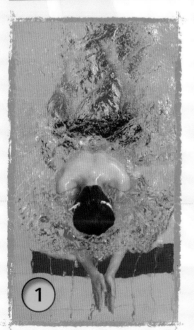

This view from above shows you how to do the kick. Bend your knees.

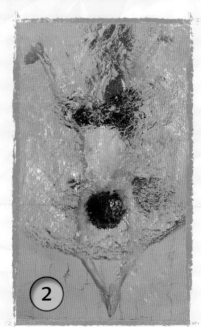

Kick out your legs powerfully behind you. You can feel the force pushing you along in the water.

11

Front Crawl

Front crawl is the fastest stroke . It feels very powerful as you move through the water.

For front crawl, swim on the surface with your face in the water and your eyes looking slightly ahead. Be **streamlined**, as though you are swimming through a narrow tube.

Legs
Do long fast kicks, using your whole leg. Your knees should bend a little and your feet should make a small splash. Your big toes should be almost touching each other as they kick.

Arms

Your arms provide the power in front crawl. With one arm out in front, start to lift the other arm.

Lift your elbow high out of the water at 90 degrees from your body. Keep your hand near the water.

Put your hand in the water in front of your head and stretch it forwards as far as it will go. Slice the water with your thumb first. The less splash the better.

Bend your elbow and push your hand towards your feet, until it reaches the top of your leg. Straighten your elbow as your hand reaches your hip.

Lift your other arm out of the water. As you turn your head to the side you can take a breath.

TRY THIS

It is often hard to get the hang of the breathing at first. Practise breathing in different ways. If you usually breathe every two strokes on your right hand side, try to practise breathing every three strokes. This will help you to swim better and faster.

Turn your head smoothly, resting the side of your head in the water.

Backstroke

The backstroke is different than most strokes because you can't see where you are going!

It is a good idea to count how many strokes it takes you to swim a length so you will know when you are getting close to the end of the pool. Try to swim with all of your body close to the surface of the water, like you are lying on your back in bed with your head on a pillow.

The arms provide the power in backstroke. Start to bring your left arm out of the water. Keep your arm straight. The left and right arms do the same movement, but not at the same time. One should come out of the water at around the same time as the other enters it.

Bring your left arm up. **Rotate** your wrist so your hand is flat. Bring your left arm down so it has made a semi-circle above the water.

Continue rotating your wrist so your little finger will go into the water first. Keep your left arm straight. Continue circling your right arm.

As your left arm hits the water, your right arm should start to lift above the surface.

Lift your right arm out of the water, with your palm facing your leg. Your thumb should break the surface first. Use long fast kicks, with your knees underwater and slightly bent. Your toes should make a small splash as you kick.

TRY THIS

Keep your chin tucked in close to your chest to help to improve your speed. Keeping your head still will also increase your speed through the water. Some coaches put a coin on a swimmer's forehead to see if they can keep it there for a whole length!

Tucking your chin in and keeping your head still makes you more streamlined.

Butterfly

Butterfly requires stamina and technique. Both of your arms work at the same time and keep moving all through the stroke.

The dolphin-like motion of the body through the water is known as **undulation**. It helps push you through the water. Keep your legs close and turn your feet in slightly to make them like the tail of a dolphin.

Put your hands in the water in front of your shoulders and pull them under water towards your feet. Kick your legs down as your hands go in. Keep your head down when your arms go over the water. Keep your head in the water, except when you need to breathe in.

Kick your legs down again as your hands come out. Keep your head down until your arms are near your thighs. Lift your chin and breathe in quickly. When your hands reach your thighs, lift them out of the water and throw them back to the start.

TRY THIS

To breathe, try pushing your chin forwards so your mouth comes out of the water. It is best to do this when your arms are almost at your thighs. If you lift your head up at other times it is difficult to get your arms over.

The photographs below show a top view of how to move your arms. When you lift your arms out of the water, keep them as near to the water as possible. Throw them forwards in a wide and low arc. Put your hands in the water with your palms facing outwards so the thumbs go in first, with the elbows slightly bent. Every time you pull with your arms, you should kick twice. The order is kick, pull the arms, kick, throw your arms over.

A good start gets you into the water quickly and smoothly. Think safety! Never dive until you have checked the water is deep enough.

The Grab Start

The grab start gives a swimmer a powerful dive into the pool.

1 Keep your head tucked in close to your knees. Raise your hips. Curl your toes over the edge of the block and bend your knees slightly. Grip the block by placing your palms on the front surface.

2 Push off powerfully. Throw your arms forwards.

3 Tuck your head in, push your hips up and streamline your body, so you enter the water head first.

The Track Start

The track start is more stable than the grab start and with a strong push off you can dive further into the water.

Place one foot back on the starting block and the other foot forwards. Hold the block with your hands on either side of your front leg.

Lean forwards and pull down for an instant. Throw your head and arms forwards. Drive with your legs and perform a shallow dive.

Backstroke Start

Backstroke is the only swimming style with a different start.

Face the wall and hold the start block or the wall with your hands. Place your legs on the wall with both heels slightly raised. Just before the start, pull your head closer to the start block. Keep your knees bent at a 90 degree angle. On the signal to start, clasp your hands together. Push off with your legs and bring your arms above your head. Your bottom should hit the water first.

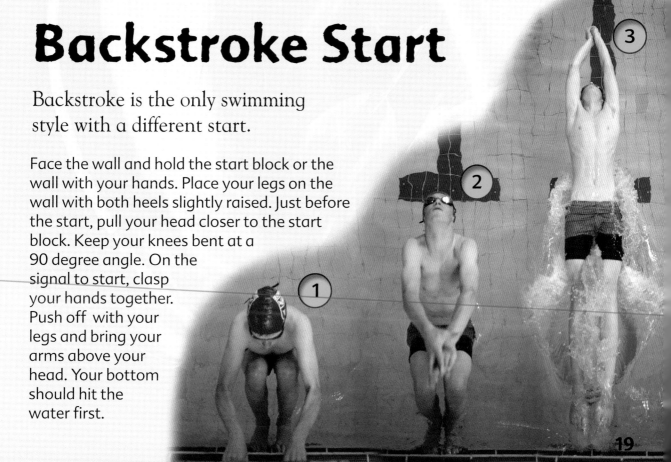

Flip Turns

The flip turn allows you to finish one length and begin the next as fast as possible.

In competitions, any part of your body can touch the wall, so use your feet to get the fastest turn.

The flip turn is basically a somersault and twist. Swim quickly toward the wall. You will need some **momentum** to make the turn.

If your pool has lanes drawn on the floor, start to turn when you see the 'T' on the bottom of your lane. Make sure you have plenty of air in your lungs when you start to turn.

Tuck your head in tight and keep kicking your legs so that you roll forwards in the water. As you flip, breathe out hard through your nose to prevent any water getting up it.

Your momentum should mean your legs follow you around the turn. This is why it is important to swim quickly towards the wall in step 1.

(5)

Place both feet firmly on the wall and push off hard under water. For front strokes turn on to your front before you surface or do any kicking. Start to twist on to your front as you push away from the wall.

You do a flip turn for front crawl and backstroke. Unlike a front stroke where you twist underwater so you are the right way up for your next length, in backstroke you do not perform the twist. Instead, you need to roll onto your front before you start to do the turn. Throw your arm over your opposite shoulder to roll.

TRY THIS

It is difficult to find the wall when approaching a turn doing backstroke. You can count how many strokes it takes to get from one end to the other. You need to leave space to turn on to your front and then to flip, so don't count all the way to the end of the pool.

For backstroke, remain on your back as you push away.

LIFESAVING

Some swimmers learn skills that can help others. Lifeguards need to learn lifesaving skills. It is important that all swimmers know how to help themselves and others if they get in trouble in the water, too.

Swimmers and lifeguards use a safety phrase, 'talk, reach, throw, row, go' to show the order you should follow if you see someone in difficulty. Talk to the person in the water first. Your advice may help them get to a safe place if they are calm enough. Reach for them with your hand, or a pole if they are near and there is no danger of them pulling you in. If they are too far away, throw them a life preserver or rope to pull them in with. If they are in a lake or the ocean, look for a boat you can use to reach them. Only enter the water and attempt a rescue as a last resort. You will ideally be a strong swimmer and a trained lifesaver.

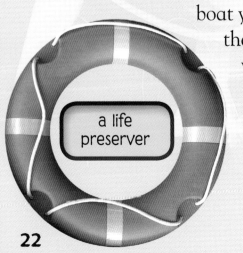

a life preserver

This chin tow is a good rescue hold. It reassures a struggling swimmer because you stay close. Lean backwards, and cup the struggling swimmer's chin in the palm of your hand. Get in a sitting position, keeping your legs clear so you don't kick the person that you are rescuing.

Start to travel along the water by moving your legs and arm.

Make scissor movements with your legs to move yourself along. Make **sculling** movements with your free arm, changing the angle of your hands while sweeping your arms back and forth to propel you.

Keep reassuring the person you are rescuing.

TRY THIS

Why not join a lifesaving class at your local pool?

23

WATER POLO

Water polo is played in a swimming pool. Two teams of seven players play in a water polo match. The aim is to score goals.

Players pass a ball by throwing it to one another. They try to throw, push or carry the ball into a net to score a goal. The goalkeepers are the only players who can touch the ball with both hands. All the other players can only touch the ball with one hand. Players must not touch the bottom or sides of the pool.

Water polo players wear caps with their numbers on them. The home team wears white caps, the away team wears blue and the goalkeepers wear red caps.

Eggbeater Kick

The eggbeater kick is used in **synchronised** swimming and water polo to keep swimmers afloat in an upright position. Swimmers make alternating circular movements of the legs to produce an upwards force and keep them afloat.

Move both your legs in a circular motion. One leg goes **clockwise** while the other leg goes **anticlockwise**, like the action of a whisk.

You can now use your arms to throw and catch in water polo. In between the action you can scull your hands to help stay afloat.

TRY THIS

A water polo pool is deep enough to prevent swimmers from touching or pushing off from the bottom. Swimmers are not allowed to touch the sides either. You have to be a strong swimmer to just stay afloat for a session, let alone compete. Water polo has four seven-minute quarters. Try treading water for seven minutes to see if you can do it. Keep the edge within an arm's reach in case you get tired.

The Throw

Water polo players need to be able to catch and throw. Experienced players can catch and release a pass with a single motion.

A water polo ball is around the same size as a football. It has a rubbery feel and can be gripped in one hand. If you squeeze the ball too tightly it will pop out of your hand. Grip the ball with the thumb and little finger and let the three inside fingers guide the throw. When passing, your wrist should bend forwards and back, not twist to the side.

TRY THIS

Keep your eyes on the target and throw from your shoulder. If you are right handed have your left shoulder forwards. As you pass the ball, your left shoulder should turn sharply to the left. Your right shoulder should turn forwards and to the left.

Hold the ball in the air behind your head with your elbow raised. If your elbow hits the water, the pass is slower and less accurate. As you throw, turn your body in the direction of the target. Let the ball roll off your fingertips and snap your wrist forwards, slapping the water in front of you.

The Catch

Hold your hand up to make a target for the person passing you the ball. Watch the pass to see if you need to swim to get to it.

Use your eggbeater kick to get high out of the water. Splay your fingers out to receive the pass.

Relax your arm as the ball hits your hand. The weight of the ball and the momentum will carry your arm back.

Bend your elbow and swing your shoulder back to hold the ball behind your head with your hand beneath it. The momentum of the pass carries your arm back into the ready position.

From this position you can easily shoot, pass or put the ball in the water to swim.

TRY DIVING

If you have a head for heights, you might like to try diving. Learn with an instructor before you head for a high board. It can be as dangerous as it looks!

A dive breaks down into three main phases, takeoff, flight and entry. The aim is to link the three as gracefully as possible and to enter the water with a straight body and little splash. Divers can take off facing forwards or backwards. For forward takeoffs, divers can run along the board or take off from a standing position. For backward takeoffs, they must spring up from a standing position. For platform dives, there is also the option of taking off from a handstand.

A handstand and a backward facing takeoff position

a tuck

a pike

In flight, a diver can adopt different positions. They can dive straight, in a pike, in a tuck, do a twist or do a combination of these. The diver must enter the water as **vertical** as possible. They should have a straight body, their feet together and their toes pointed. For feet-first entries, their straight arms should be close to the body.

For a back or reverse dive, slightly arch your body before entering the water. Try not to make a splash.

TRY THIS

Practise your arm position. Your arms should be over your head and in line with your body. Your hands can be on top of each other, as in this photo, or clasped to make a flat surface to hit the water. This reduces the splash.

GLOSSARY

anticlockwise In the opposite direction to which the hands of a clock turn

cardiovascular Relating to, or involving the heart and blood vessels

clockwise In the direction that the hands of a clock turn

endurance The ability to withstand hardship, adversity or stress

freestyle A competition, such as a swimming race, in which the competitors are not restricted to a particular stroke

hypothermia Reduction of the body temperature to an abnormally low level

momentum The characteristic of a moving body caused by its mass and its motion

rotate To turn or cause to turn about an axis or a centre

sculling To move the hands in a rowing motion in order to stay afloat

stamina Endurance

streamlined Designed or constructed to make motion through water or air easier

symmetrically Being alike in size, shape and relative position on opposite sides of a dividing line

synchronised Done at the same time, such as synchronised swimmers' movements

technique A method of accomplishing a desired aim

undulation A wavy appearance or form

vertical Going straight up or down from a level surface

FOR MORE INFORMATION

Books

Apps, Roy, *Dream to Win: Ellie Simmonds* (Franklin Watts, 2013)

Heneghan, Judith, *Mad About: Swimming* (Wayland, 2016)

Hunter, Rebecca, *Starting Sport: Swimming* (Franklin Watts, 2012)

King, Chris, *Dream to Win: Tom Daley* (Franklin Watts, 2014)

Websites

BBC Get Inspired: How to get into Swimming
www.bbc.co.uk/sport/get-inspired/23164764
Gives information and advice about getting into swimming.

The Swimming Expert
theswimmingexpert.com
Expert tips and videos to help with perfecting you strokes.

The website addresses (URLs) included in this book were valid at the time of going to press. However, it is possible that contents or addresses may have changed since the publication of this book. No responsibility for any such changes can be accepted by either the author or the Publisher.

INDEX

backstroke 8, 14, 15, 21
backstroke start 19
breaststroke 8, 10
butterfly 8, 16, 17

canoeing 4

diving 28, 29
doggy paddle 8

eggbeater kick 25, 27

flip turns 20, 21
front crawl 8, 9, 12, 13

grab start 18

lifeguards 4, 22
life preservers 22
lifesaving 4, 9, 22, 23

pike 29

sidestroke 8, 9
surfing 4

track start 19
travel stroke 8
treading water 8
trudgen 8
tuck 29
twist 29

warm-ups 6, 7
water polo 24, 25
water polo catch 27
water polo throw 26
waterskiing 4
windsurfing 4